IMAGES
of America

WICHITA FALLS

The natives of North Texas lived in grass-thatched shelters such as this one before the coming of the white man. This picture was probably taken in the 1890s. (Courtesy of the Wichita Falls Museum of Art at Midwestern State University.)

ON THE COVER: By 1919, as a result of the oil boom, the population of Wichita Falls had soared to nearly 40,000. Many of the city's residents turned out to welcome home the veterans of the Great War, which had ended with the armistice of November 11, 1918. This picture was taken from the corner of Eighth and Indiana Streets looking toward Seventh Street. (Courtesy of the Wichita Falls Museum of Art at Midwestern State University.)

IMAGES
of America

WICHITA FALLS

Kenneth E. Hendrickson Jr.

ARCADIA
PUBLISHING

Published by Arcadia Publishing
Charleston, South Carolina

Library of Congress Control Number: 2009930177

For all general information contact Arcadia Publishing at:
Telephone 843-853-2070
Fax 843-853-0044
E-mail sales@arcadiapublishing.com
For customer service and orders:
Toll-Free 1-888-313-2665

Visit us on the Internet at www.arcadiapublishing.com

*This book is dedicated to the memory of Joseph A. Kemp
and Frank Kell, whose contributions to the growth and
development of Wichita Falls were enormous.*

CONTENTS

ACKNOWLEDGMENTS

Most of the images in this book come from two sources: the Wichita Falls *Times Record News* and the Wichita Falls Museum of Art at Midwestern State University. The images from the latter are from the Lester Jones Collection. In addition, several photographs were contributed by the author.

This project could not have been completed without the cooperation of the good people at the newspaper and the museum, and the author owes them a special thank-you. At the *Times Record News*, editor Deanna Watson and archivist Jill Sexton were most helpful, as were director Cohn Drennan and curator Danny Bills at the museum. At Arcadia Publishing, assistance and encouragement were provided by Kristie Kelly and Luke Cunningham. Their support and encouragement during the research process, always stressful for an author, were very much appreciated. However, it was graduate student and technical assistant Kara Sullivan, who did all the scanning and typing, who brought life to this book. Without her help, Images of America: *Wichita Falls* would not exist. Finally, a friendly thank-you goes to Annetta Reusch of Wichita Falls High School, who provided vital information about "Old High."

INTRODUCTION

The site of Wichita Falls in the North Texas grasslands just east of the hundredth meridian was the traditional homeland of nomadic Native American tribes, notably the Kiowa and Comanche. In the years following the Civil War, cattlemen began to invade the area in search of grazing for their herds, and by the late 1870s, permanent settlers appeared. By 1882, several of these hardy folks had established homes near the Wichita River and made their living by farming or selling needed supplies to the cattlemen. On September 27, 1882, the Texas Townsite Company held a town lot sale and Wichita Falls was born. This event would not have taken place except for the fact that the Fort Worth and Denver City Railroad had agreed to extend its line right through the heart of the little village.

According to local lore, the first permanent settler on the site of Wichita Falls was John H. Barwise, who arrived with his wife and five children in 1879. Barwise began his new life in the prairie town as a farmer and then created his own freight line to carry his produce to market in Henrietta, the closest town with a railroad. Barwise persevered, and by 1882, he was doing well.

The little town continued to grow during the 1880s. More settlers arrived, lured by the availability of land and the presence of the railroad. Schools, churches, and new businesses appeared, and by the 1890s, Wichita Falls was the county seat of Wichita County and had become the rail center of the entire area. In fact, more railroads had been built, and one of them, the Wichita Falls and Northwestern Railway, was a project of Joseph A. Kemp and brother-in-law Frank Kell. Over the next several decades, Kemp and Kell were to become two of the most important and successful men in the city.

Kemp had decided to settle in Wichita Falls after a brief visit in 1883 persuaded him that the town offered many possibilities, and he went to work immediately upon his arrival. At first, he supplied staple goods to farmers and ranchers, and then he went into banking and real estate. Later he developed the city's water supply system and experimented with various agricultural projects. Frank Kell worked closely with his brother-in-law on many of these projects but was primarily interested in the milling business. Shortly after his arrival, in 1897, he established his first mill, and the Wichita Mill and Elevator Company eventually became the largest operation of its kind in North Texas. Together Kemp and Kell built railroads, a lake, an irrigation system, a streetcar system, the first power company, and at least a dozen manufacturing plants of various kinds.

By 1901, Wichita Falls was a well-established community of about 5,000 souls; then came the discovery of oil. The first strike that year was in Clay County a few miles east of town. The second discovery came in 1911 near the town of Electra, located about 20 miles to the west, and the third was in 1918 near the village of Burkburnett, about 14 miles north. This one triggered a full-blown boom. The first gusher blew in on July 29, and before long, hundreds of wealth seekers descended on the area, hundreds of wells went down, and fortunes were made and lost in rapid succession. The boom would last until the early 1920s and would result in the transformation of Wichita Falls into a modern city.

One of the events that drove the boom was World War I, which broke out in Europe in 1914. In 1917, the United States entered the war and the demand for gasoline and other petroleum products escalated, but oil production was not the only contribution of Wichita Falls to the war effort. Soon after the United States entered the conflict, it was learned that the army proposed to establish more than 30 training camps in Texas, and Kemp and Kell, ever on the lookout for new projects, set out to bring one to Wichita Falls. They succeeded, and soon Call Field was in business on a 640-acre site just west of the city. Between August 1917 and July 1919, hundreds of young men were trained to fly in combat at Call Field and some 500 were commissioned. Thirty-four young cadets were killed in crashes while training at the field.

Before the oil boom, the city had experienced significant growth and development based on the agricultural economy of the area. After the boom, especially in the 1920s, growth continued at an even more frenetic pace with oil now the cornerstone of the economy. There was a building boom, a banking boom, a business boom, and a population boom. Between 1910 and 1920, the population soared from 8,000 to 40,000. Also, during the early 1920s, the school system expanded; one feature of the expansion was the creation in 1922 of a junior college that would later develop into Midwestern State University, the premier small liberal arts institution in the state.

The Great Depression hit the city hard. Businesses folded, people lost their jobs, farmers lost their farms, and the oil patch seemed to have dried up. Nevertheless, the people persevered. In 1932, the city staged an elaborate three-day Diamond Jubilee to celebrate the 50th anniversary of its founding, which was a resounding success. Then toward the end of the decade, two things happened to once again stimulate the economy: a group of gambling oil men, calling themselves the Deep Oil Production Company, hit a significant deposit in the Kemp-Munger-Allen field just east of the city in 1938; and in 1939, World War II broke out in Europe. The KMA discovery revived the oil industry and the war brought Sheppard Field, now Sheppard Air Force Base, to the city. Production in the KMA field continues today, and Sheppard became a major training site during the war, a Strategic Air Command base later, and more recently a training center for NATO pilots.

Major changes once again confronted the city in the 1950s. Oil production declined, and the companies that had established refineries in Wichita Falls in the wake of the big boom now decided to close them or move them. One by one, they disappeared until by the end of the decade there were none where once there had been 30. To meet the crisis, city leaders formed the Bureau of Commerce and Industry to recruit new businesses. By the mid-1970s, several manufacturing plants had been established, producing such diverse products as glass, clothing, and electrical components. Moreover, the oil industry showed some signs of resurgence, and Sheppard continued to expand.

Throughout the history of Wichita Falls, weather has played a major role in the lives of its people. The Wichita River and the creeks that meander throughout the city have periodically produced devastating floods, and tornadoes have struck all too often. In the last five decades, tornadoes have ravished the city on three occasions: 1958, 1964, and 1979. The 1979 storm hit the city on the evening of April 10 and was by far the most destructive. Forty-four people died, more than 2,000 were injured, and 6,000 people were homeless. Damage was estimated at $500 million, and President Carter declared the city a disaster area. After recovering from the initial shock, the people responded as they always have—with courage and resolve. Most of the structures destroyed by the tornado were replaced in record time. Wichitans believe in their city and in their motto: "The city that faith built." They never give up.

One

1870s THROUGH 1915

Quanah Parker, one of the last chiefs of the
Comanches, was the son of Cynthia Ann Parker,
who had been kidnapped by Native Americans at the
age of nine in 1836, and Peta Nocona, a Comanche
chief, whom she married in 1843. Cynthia Ann was
seized and returned to the white world in 1860 but
was very unhappy. She died in 1864. Quanah Parker
became a ferocious warrior and led his Kwahadi band
in numerous battles against the U.S. Army. He finally
surrendered to reservation life in 1875 and lived
out the rest of his days near Fort Sill in Oklahoma
Territory. He died in 1911. (Courtesy of the Wichita
Falls Museum of Art at Midwestern State University.)

Quanah Parker's favorite wife was Too Nicy, shown here with a child. The exact date of this photograph is unknown. (Courtesy of the Wichita Falls Museum of Art at Midwestern State University.)

The Kiowas roamed North Texas in quest of the buffalo, which sustained their way of life, until they were forced to move onto the reservation in 1875. After that, they frequently visited Wichita Falls. These two Kiowa girls were photographed in the city in 1890. (Courtesy of the Wichita Falls Museum of Art at Midwestern State University.)

Col. Ranald Slidell McKenzie graduated first in his class at West Point in 1862. He distinguished himself in battle during the Civil War and later served on several frontier posts, including Fort Richardson and Fort Sill. He was a leader in the Red River War (1874–1875), which resulted in the defeat of the Kiowas and the Comanches. The last Comanche leader to surrender was Quanah Parker. (Courtesy of the Wichita Falls Museum of Art at Midwestern State University.)

Doan's Store was established by Corwin and Jonathan Doan in 1878 a few miles north of Vernon on the Red River. They traded with the Native Americans and the cowboys who came by on cattle drives. Vernon is located about 50 miles west of Wichita Falls. The folks in Vernon celebrate the existence of Doan's Store with a party and ceremony every year. (Courtesy of the Wichita Falls Museum of Art at Midwestern State University.)

TOWN LOTS

IN THE TOWN OF

WICHITA FALLS,

Wichita County, Texas,

The Terminus of the

Ft. Worth & Denver City Railway,

Sept. 27,1882

WICHITA FALLS is located in the fertile valley of the Big Wichita river, in Wichita ~~nty, 115 miles from Fort Worth and about ....ve miles from where it empties into Red River, opposite the Indian Territory, in the center of one of the most beautiful and healthy sections of the Northwest. Here are located the end of the first division and the main repair and machine shops of the Ft. Worth & Denver City railway. Here are also situate the Falls and Rapids of the Big Wichita river, which make it the finest water-power and the future manufacturing center of Northwestern Texas. Good water, for domestic purposes, can be secured at a depth of from twenty to forty feet.

These advantages will enable it to control the entire trade of the southern portion of the Indian Territory and of the vast Pan Handle of Texas, and which will make it the finest cattle shipping point in the state.

TERMS OF SALE—Purchases not exceeding $100, to be paid in cash at time of purchase. Purchases exceeding $100, one-half cash, one-fourth in six months and one-fourth in twelve months from date of purchase. All deferred payments to bear ten per cent. interest from the date of sale. Vendor's lien retained to secure payment of notes. Sale to commence at 10 o'clock a. m.

EXCURSION TRAINS will be run from Ft. Wor' to Wichita Falls on the day preceding and d' ing the continuance of sale at reduced rates.

For further information and maps, apply to R. E. MONTGOMERY, General Town Lot agent, Fort Worth, Texas.

C. L. FROST, General Passenger Agent, Fort Worth, Texas.

A. H. HOSACK, Auctioneer.   sep 8 17t

This advertisement for the Wichita Falls town lot sale to be held on September 27, 1882, appeared in a San Antonio newspaper on September 8. Like most notices of its kind in those days, it exaggerates the attractions of the North Texas region. The so-called falls in the Wichita River were rapids with a drop of no more than 5 feet. (Courtesy of the Wichita Falls Museum of Art at Midwestern State University.)

R. E. Montgomery, son-in-law of railroad builder Grenville Dodge, conducted the first auction of town lots in Wichita Falls on September 7, 1882. The first lot, located on Ohio Avenue, sold for $1,200, but most went for prices between $200 and $500. On the same day, the Fort Worth and Denver City Railroad reached the town, and the stage was set for economic development. (Courtesy of the Wichita Falls Museum of Art at Midwestern State University.)

Joseph A. Kemp came to Wichita Falls in 1883. His first business endeavor was a wholesale grocery, which was successful and soon had branch offices in several nearby towns. Kemp's most important customers were ranchers. When the City National Bank was organized, he became its president and was later chairman of the board for many years. Among his other business ventures were railroads; a truck company; Lakes Wichita, Kemp, and Diversion; the public library; and a streetcar system. He also inaugurated an irrigation system that he worked on for a quarter of a century. The goal of this project was the development of truck farming in the Wichita Falls area, but it was never consummated. This picture was taken in 1884. (Courtesy of the Wichita Falls Museum of Art at Midwestern State University.)

This picture of Joseph A Kemp was taken in the 1920s when he was at the height of his career. His face reflects feelings of success and contentment. Note the diamond stick pin in his tie. (Courtesy of the Wichita Falls *Times Record News*.)

Frank Kell married Lulu Kemp, sister of Joseph A. Kemp, in 1885. His primary business interest was grain and milling, and he was successful and well known in central Texas. In 1897, at the urging of his brother-in-law, he moved to Wichita Falls and established the Wichita Mill and Elevator Company. His business continued to expand until, at one time, he owned nine mills and more than 100 country elevators. He sold his properties to General Mills in 1928. Kell also partnered with Joseph Kemp in numerous business ventures and civil activities. (Courtesy of the Wichita Falls Museum of Art at Midwestern State University.)

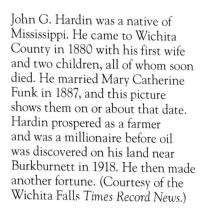

John G. Hardin was a native of Mississippi. He came to Wichita County in 1880 with his first wife and two children, all of whom soon died. He married Mary Catherine Funk in 1887, and this picture shows them on or about that date. Hardin prospered as a farmer and was a millionaire before oil was discovered on his land near Burkburnett in 1918. He then made another fortune. (Courtesy of the Wichita Falls *Times Record News.*)

It has long been debated whether the Panhandle National Bank or the Exchange Bank was the first bank in Wichita Falls. Both opened for businesses in 1884. In this photograph, taken in that year, Mr. Israel, owner of the Exchange Bank, is seen standing second from the left. To his right and from left to right, are Joe McFarland, Henry Stanley, and the bank manager, Mr. Archibald. The identities of the other men in the picture are unknown. (Courtesy of the Wichita Falls *Times Record News*.)

This 1885 view of the Ward and Stanley General Store includes, from left to right, J. P. Ward, C. E. Z. Reid, Will Estes, and John Strange. (Courtesy of the Wichita Falls *Times Record News*.)

In 1885, three years after the first town sale, the village of Wichita Falls looked like this. The large structure just left of center in the photograph is the courthouse. (Courtesy of the Wichita Falls *Times Record News*.)

The Ward and Stanley general store was built in 1884 at the corner of Eighth and Ohio Streets. This scene is from 1886. Note the unpaved streets and the absence of electric wires. (Courtesy of the Wichita Falls *Times Record News*.)

This building was originally constructed in the early 1880s and stood in the 700 block of Lamar Street. It was used as a courthouse. In 1885, it was moved to Tenth and Scott Streets and was used as a schoolhouse until 1890. (Courtesy of the Wichita Falls Museum of Art at Midwestern State University.)

This is an important picture made in 1886. It reflects the melding of commerce and rural life. In the background is the Panhandle National Bank, one of the city's first banks, founded by John James. In the foreground are area cattlemen who were customers of the bank. (Courtesy of the Wichita Falls Museum of Art at Midwestern State University.)

O. W. Bean and his son Burt stand behind the counter of the O. W. Bean and Son Store in 1889. The man in front of them is a salesman. Note that the store is well stocked and offers everything from Ivory soap to crackers. (Courtesy of the Wichita Falls *Times Record News*.)

This is the M. F. Yager home pictured in 1889, the year it was built. It was a substantial structure, suggesting that at least some of the residents of the new town were prosperous. The house was located at 1704 Travis Street and stood until 1919. (Courtesy of the Wichita Falls *Times Record News*.)

This picture, taken from the roof of the courthouse in 1890, shows a portion of the business district. Note the churches and the buildings under construction. (Courtesy of the Wichita Falls *Times Record News*.)

This picture, made about 1905 or 1906, shows the Fashion Stable, which was located on the East side of Indiana Avenue, between Seventh and Eighth Streets.

E. B. Gorsline and his wife, Olive, arrived in Wichita Falls in the late 1880s. At first, Gorsline tried the bakery business but soon established the Fashion Stable. He became famous as one of the most knowledgeable horsemen in the area and remained in business until automobiles began to supplant horses and buggies. He then went into the real estate business and was once again successful. (Courtesy of the Wichita Falls *Times Record News*.)

These ladies were the first graduates of Wichita Falls High School. From left to right, they are Nevie Watts, Bessie Woodhouse, and Callie Robinson. (Courtesy of Annetta Reusch at Wichita Falls High School.)

In the early 1890s, the population of Wichita Falls was about 2,000 and the town had already developed a bustling business district. This scene on Ohio Avenue features the Kerr and Hursh Brothers Hardware Store, the Wichita *Herald* (the town's first newspaper), and a portion of Kahn's Furniture Store. (Courtesy of the Wichita Falls *Times Record News*.)

Boardinghouses were common as more and more settlers arrived in town. Pictured here is the Warner Boardinghouse as it appeared in 1890. Note that meals could be had for 25¢. (Courtesy of the Wichita Falls *Times Record News*.)

This boardinghouse was located in the 1100 block on Indiana Avenue in the 1890s. It was owned and operated by Mrs. Charley Young, who is standing at the far right. (Courtesy of the Wichita Falls *Times Record News*.)

The boardinghouse business was good to the Young family, and they built a more elaborate structure around the turn of the 20th century. This building is evocative of Victorian prosperity. (Courtesy of the Wichita Falls *Times Record News*.)

As businesses expanded in Wichita Falls, hotels began to appear to serve the needs of cattlemen and salesmen. This hotel, the Mansion, was built in 1892 and featured baths and a restaurant. Located on Indiana Avenue, it was in operation for many years. (Courtesy of the Wichita Falls *Times Record News*.)

Robert E. Huff arrived in Wichita Falls in 1882 on his way to Vernon but was invited to stay by J. H. Barwise. Here he practiced law and was involved in numerous civic and business activities. He was a member of the first Board of Trustees of Education and served as a city alderman. In 1888, he was made a director of Panhandle National Bank, was elected president in the same year, and served in that capacity until 1920. He also was president of the City Bar and president of the chamber of commerce. He was a delegate to the Democratic National Convention on four occasions, and in 1912, at Baltimore, he was one of the "Texas 40" who supported Woodrow Wilson on every ballot. (Courtesy of the Wichita Falls *Times Record News*.)

This majestic Victorian structure, the home of the R. E. Huff family, was built in 1892. Seated on the front porch is part of the family. The Huffs had seven children, four sons and three daughters. All the girls died young, and their youngest boy died in 1920. (Courtesy of the Wichita Falls *Times Record News*.)

These Confederate veterans gathered for a reunion in Wichita Falls in 1894. Presumably, they were all Texans, although that cannot be verified. (Courtesy of the Wichita Falls *Times Record News*.)

This photograph was taken in the front office of the City National Bank in 1895. Seated on the left is C. A. Brown, vice president of the bank, and on the right is cashier Frank Dorsey. Little did Dorsey know that he had less than a year to live. (Courtesy of the Wichita Falls *Times Record News*.)

Horses were important in the lives of most Wichitans until well into the 20th century. Facilities such as the J. S. Fore Feed and Livery Stable served the needs of both horses and their owners. This picture was taken in 1895. (Courtesy of the Wichita Falls *Times Record News.*)

Before the discovery of oil, agriculture dominated the economy in Wichita County, and Wichita Falls was the marketing center. In this picture, farmers are preparing their field for planting winter wheat in the fall of 1900. (Courtesy of the Wichita Falls *Times Record News.*)

In this image, farmers are harvesting winter wheat in the spring of 1900. (Courtesy of the Wichita Falls *Times Record News*.)

The Fort Worth and Denver City Railroad, built by Grenville Dodge, was the first line to arrive in Wichita Falls in 1882. Myron Barwise, son of J. H. Barwise, became a railroad engineer and is seen here standing in the cab doorway of a Fort Worth and Denver City locomotive. (Courtesy of the Wichita Falls *Times Record News*.)

Interior scene in City National Bank about 1896. Reading from left to right:
W. L. Robertson, L. P. Webb, Mr. Wheeler, P. P. Langford, and O. E. Cannon.

This picture of the interior of the City National Bank may have been taken at some date after February 25, 1896, because cashier Frank Dorsey, who was killed in a robbery on that date, is not there. Those present from left to right are W. L. Robertson, L. P. Webb, Mr. Weller, P. P. Langford, and O. E. Cannon. (Courtesy of the Wichita Falls *Times Record News*.)

The City National Bank opened for business on March 6, 1890, at the corner of Seventh and Indiana Streets. On February 25, 1896, the bank was robbed by two cowboys, Foster Crawford and Elmer Lewis. Cashier Frank Dorsey attempted to foil the robbery but was shot and killed by one of the bandits. Dorsey appears at the right in this picture, which was taken earlier in 1896. (Courtesy of the Wichita Falls *Times Record News*.)

Frank Dorsey, cashier of the City National Bank, had a wife and three children. The bandits who killed him, Foster Crawford and Elmer Lewis, were captured and put in jail, but they were soon dragged out by an angry mob and lynched. No charges were ever filed, but the reward money was paid and most of it was given to Dorsey's widow. (Courtesy of the Wichita Falls Museum of Art at Midwestern State University.)

The county jailhouse is pictured here in 1896. The people on the steps are Mrs. L. B. Hardesty and her three children. Those standing below, from left to right, are jailer Frank Hardesty, deputy George Giddings, county clerk ? Reid, assistant county clerk Walter Reid, janitor Tom Arthur, county judge Edgar Scurry, and deputy sheriff Sam Abbot. It was from this building that the two bandits, Foster Crawford and Elmer Lewis, were snatched and lynched. (Courtesy of the Wichita Falls Museum of Art at Midwestern State University.)

In the early days of its development, alcohol was easily available in Wichita Falls and the town was known to thirsty men as "Whiskey Taw Falls." Two of the many saloons that graced the downtown district are shown here. (Courtesy of the Wichita Falls *Times Record News*.)

This is the T. H. Wilson Grocery Store as it appeared in 1897. Note that it appears to be well stocked, but the store was probably not very clean by modern standards. All the items for sale would have been brought in by train. (Courtesy of the Wichita Falls *Times Record News*.)

This is the real estate office of J. W. Stone. Obviously, they took their work very seriously. (Courtesy of the Wichita Falls *Times Record News*.)

The Wichita Valley Railroad was a project of Grenville Dodge and Morgan Jones in 1890. Pictured here is locomotive No. 38 and part of the crew. Engineer Myron Barwise stands third from the right leaning against the locomotive. (Courtesy of the Wichita Falls *Times Record News*.)

Meet the fourth and fifth graders in Wichita School, class of 1901. On the far left is teacher Mrs. O. R. Dunn, and on the far right is Supt. W. F. Jourdan. (Courtesy of the Wichita Falls Museum of Art at Midwestern State University.)

The Wichita Drug House was one of many successful businesses in the early 20th century. It was located at 607 Seventh Street. Pictured here from left to right are pharmacist G. R. Wallace, owner Dr. J. F. Reed, and Dr. A. A. Jones, who maintained an office in the back of the store. Note that tobacco products are prominently displayed in the front counter. (Courtesy of the Wichita Falls *Times Record News.*)

This early-20th-century clothing store featured a nice selection for both men and women. (Courtesy of the Wichita Falls *Times Record News.*)

This is Bud Long's meat market as it appeared in the early 20th century. The exact date is unknown and the identities of the young men in the picture have been lost, but the picture has some interesting features. Note that the market had electricity and a cold box (behind the cash register), but the counter was homemade and the floor needs sweeping. The portion of the floor behind the counter and under the cutting table was covered with sawdust. One can only hope that the meat on the cutting table had not been sitting out too long. (Courtesy of the Wichita Falls *Times Record News*.)

In addition to wheat, the farmers in the Wichita Falls area produced cotton and oats. In this picture, taken on July 17, 1903, farmers have brought their oat crop to town for sale. (Courtesy of the Wichita Falls *Times Record News*.)

The Wichita Broom Manufacturing Company, founded by T. B. Noble in 1902, eventually became one of the largest broom companies in the United States. (Courtesy of the Wichita Falls *Times Record News.*)

Seen here are some of the employees of the Wichita Broom Manufacturing Company. They were members of the International Broom Makers Union, an affiliate of the American Federation of Labor. (Courtesy of the Wichita Falls *Times Record News.*)

Another of the many businesses flourishing in Wichita Falls in the early 20th century was the North Texas Furniture and Coffin Company, owned and operated by John W. Bradley, shown here third from the left. The identities of the other men in the picture are unknown. (Courtesy of the Wichita Falls *Times Record News*.)

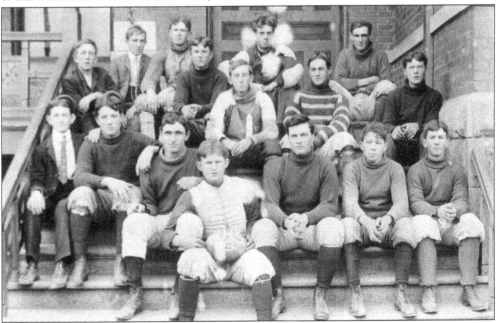

Wichita Falls High School's first football team took the field in 1903. The players are, from left to right, (first row) Joe Jones, Don McCauley, Roy Coyton, Ed Scott, Clarence Davis, Vessa Brashear, and Jim Smith; (second row) Oral Jones, Percy Hilburn, Frank Smith, Frank Hodges, Joe McDonald, Hubert Glasscock, Clyde Robertson, Everett Stonecipher, and Charles Parker. (Courtesy of the Wichita Falls Museum of Art at Midwestern State University.)

A group of Wichita Falls teachers posed for this portrait in 1904. From left to right are (first row) Myrtle Coffield, Virgie Withers, superintendant W. F. Jourdan, Merle Mann, and Emma Childers; (second row) Maggie Brothers, Bertha Taylor, Docia Shaw, Lulu Hyatt, Mr. Mullins, Maud Webb, and Ennie Phillips. (Courtesy of the Wichita Falls *Times Record News*.)

In 1904, three years after the discovery of oil in Clay County, a village known as Oil City was founded in the area. The name was soon changed to Petrolia, and this oil well supply company in Petrolia was operated by men from Wichita Falls. (Courtesy of the Wichita Falls Museum of Art at Midwestern State University.)

36

This is the home of Judge J. H. Barwise as it appeared in 1904. Judge Barwise is the bearded gentleman in the center. On the far left is Will Carrigan and on the right are Mrs. A. H. Carrigan, Ann Carrigan, and Joe Carrigan. Judge Barwise and his family settled in Wichita Falls in 1879. Although technically they were not the first settlers in the village since there were one or two other people there at the time, Barwise came to be known as the "Father of Wichita Falls" for his vision and foresight. Upon their arrival, he told his wife, Lucy, "I see a large city, prosperous with many people. Near me, I see many tall buildings which mark the business section of the city. Surrounding this is a beautiful residential section with lovely homes and paved streets," according to Jonnie Morgan's *History of Wichita Falls* (1971). (Courtesy of the Wichita Falls *Times Record News*.)

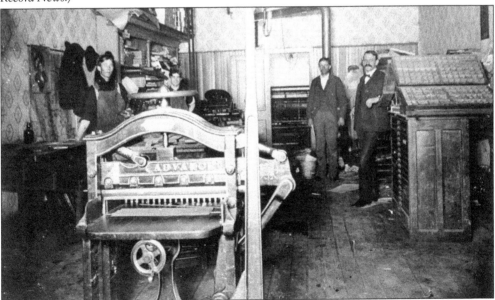

Ed Howard arrived in Wichita Falls in 1891. He acquired the *Wichita Weekly Times* in 1898 and made it a daily in 1907. In this photograph is the *Times* print shop as it appeared in 1905. (Courtesy of the Wichita Falls *Times Record News*.)

In 1905, Pres. Theodore Roosevelt came to Wichita Falls for a wolf hunt after attending a reunion of his Rough Riders in San Antonio. Cattleman Burk Burnett and other prominent figures hosted the hunt, which took place north of the Red River near Fredrick, Oklahoma. Roosevelt's party found no wolves, but they caught 17 coyotes. (Courtesy of the Wichita Falls Museum of Art at Midwestern State University.)

Before embarking on his famous wolf hunt in 1905, Pres. Theodore Roosevelt addressed a large crowd at the Wichita Falls railroad station. (Courtesy of the Wichita Falls *Times Record News*.)

The great wolf hunt took place in May 1905. Pictured here is the hunting party. From left to right are (seated) two unidentified troopers from Fort Sill, R. L. More, Guy Waggoner, Quanah Parker, Cecil Lions, Dr. Alexander Lambert, and D. P. "Fhy" Taylor; (standing) Lee Bivens, W. J. "Bill" McDonald, Jack Abernathy (famed for his ability to catch wolves with his bare hands), Gen. S. B. Young, Burk Burnett, President Roosevelt, and L. M. Gillis. (Courtesy of the Wichita Falls *Times Record News*.)

Cotton farmers brought their crop to town one Saturday in the fall of 1905. They stopped in front of the Cream Bakery and Confectionery in the 600 block of Seventh Street. Vic Stampfli, owner of the bakery and a prominent businessman, came out and is shown standing on top of a load of cotton in the right center of the picture. (Courtesy of the Wichita Falls Museum of Art at Midwestern State University.)

All well-dressed women wore hats in the early 20th century. This millinery shop served the needs of Wichita Falls ladies in 1905. (Courtesy of the Wichita Falls *Times Record News.*)

Occasionally it snows in North Texas, and when it does, Wichitans have always gone out to play. Here Ed and Olive Gorsline ride their converted sleigh past their business, the Fashion Stables, in 1905. (Courtesy of the Wichita Falls Museum of Art at Midwestern State University.)

The first automobile repair shop in Wichita Falls was opened by Alex Glass in 1907. The cars seen here belonged to T. B. Noble, J. C. Dorsey, and J. W. Stone. Stone is in the driver's seat of the car at the right, and Alex Glass is seated in the rear. The repair shop was located at Sixth and Ohio Streets. (Courtesy of the Wichita Falls *Times Record News*.)

The Wills Automobile Company was opened for business in 1907 at Seventh and Ohio Streets by Iva Wills. It was both a repair shop and a sales agency. Wills sold both Buicks and Maxwells. Frank Kell, among other prominent Wichitans, was a customer. (Courtesy of the Wichita Falls *Times Record News*.)

The Wichita Falls telephone office was located in the old City National Bank building at Seventh and Ohio Streets. The women shown here were operators in the city's first telephone exchange. Long-distance calls were possible, and the long-distance operators are seated at the right. The year was 1907. (Courtesy of the Wichita Falls *Times Record News*.)

This photograph from about 1907 features the G. W. Filgo Market located in the 800 block of Indiana Avenue. The man behind the counter on the left is employee Fritz Hendricks. Perhaps he is thinking about how he could persuade the lady in front to buy oysters. (Courtesy of the Wichita Falls *Times Record News*.)

By 1907, Frank Kell's Wichita Falls Mill was only one of his many facilities in that industry. Pictured here are some of his employees. Unfortunately, their identities are unknown. (Courtesy of the Wichita Falls *Times Record News*.)

The first professional baseball team in Wichita Falls was the Wichita Falls Cremos (named for the cigar company that sponsored them). They are shown here enjoying a send-off to play in Quanah on Labor Day 1905. (Courtesy of the Wichita Falls Museum of Art at Midwestern State University.)

Sports were popular in Wichita Falls in the early 20th century. One of the first baseball teams was a group known as the Irish Lads who played at the Lake Wichita Ballpark. Most of the players were recruited by Palmer Clark, also on the team. Pictured here was the 1910 team. Seated in front is Tubby Courtney, the team mascot. From left to right are Eddy Roher, manager and center field; J. S. Hancock, pitcher; E. J. Humphries, shortstop; Streeter Taylor, second base; W. D. Thebo, pitcher and infielder; Palmer Clark, utility; Charles Farley, first base; Frank Gibson, catcher; G. W. Guthrie, left field; Joe Bush, pitcher; Bobby Myers, pitcher; Dick Naylor, catcher; Fred Morris, pitcher; and Art Naylor, right field. Frank Gibson went on to play for the Detroit Tigers in the major leagues. (Courtesy of the Wichita Falls *Times Record News*.)

Pictured here are the Wichita Falls Drillers of 1913. From left to right, they are Nels Jones, pitcher; Fred Moms, pitcher and outfielder; Bobby Myers, pitcher; ? Randel, pitcher; ? Kizzon, first base and outfield; W. L. Guthrie, left field; Muncie Beckham, first base; Bill Baxter, pitcher; ? Phillips, second base; ? Chapman, catcher; "Pep" Clark, shortstop; ? Brown, right field; Tobbey White, catcher; and "Squire" Lawrence, third base. (Courtesy of the Wichita Falls *Times Record News*.)

Wichita Falls was a segregated community in the early 20th century, but African Americans were allowed their own amusements. Unfortunately, the identities of the baseball players in this picture, taken in the 1920s, are unknown. (Courtesy of the Wichita Falls Museum of Art at Midwestern State University.)

This is Wichita Falls' first uniformed fire department standing in front of the first city hall, located at Ninth and Ohio Streets. Chief Vic Stampfli is seated to the right of the wagon driver. This photograph was probably taken sometime between 1907 and 1910. (Courtesy of the Wichita Falls *Times Record News*.)

This picture of downtown Wichita Falls dates from 1906. It was taken at the corner of Seventh Street and Indiana Avenue facing east. At this early date, the city was already a center of business activities and prosperity even though the streets remained unpaved. (Courtesy of the Wichita Falls Museum of Art at Midwestern State University.)

Five years later, in 1911, the streetcar system had been added, but the streets were still not paved. (Courtesy of the Wichita Falls Museum of Art at Midwestern State University.)

Wichitans have always loved to celebrate holidays with a parade. In this picture is an entry in the Fourth of July Parade of 1906. Mrs. Tom W. Roberts, sister of famed cattleman Burk Burnett, holds the reins, and Sadie Kell, daughter of Frank Kell, is by her side. Sadie later married Orville Bullington, a prominent lawyer. This parade took place on Ohio Avenue, which was the city's main thoroughfare at the time. (Courtesy of the Wichita Falls *Times Record News*.)

These fine-looking young people were the graduating class of Wichita Falls High School in 1907. At that time, the population was about 5,000. There were 3 schools, 10 saloons, 14 grocery stores, 5 restaurants, and 9 churches. Except for school, which of those establishments might these youngsters have been likely to frequent? (Courtesy of the Wichita Falls *Times Record News*.)

Vic Stampfli was a successful businessman in Wichita Falls early in the 20th century. He was owner and operator of the Cream Bakery and Confectionery, located at 617 Seventh Street, and also chief of the volunteer fire department. He is shown here standing behind the counter of his establishment in 1908. (Courtesy of the Wichita Falls *Times Record News*.)

The first firefighters in Wichita Falls were members of a volunteer group organized in 1892. J. L. McClure became the first paid fireman in 1907. All the rest were volunteers, including fire chief Vic Stampfli. Here the firemen are showing off their first motorized fire engine. The year is 1910. (Courtesy of the Wichita Falls *Times Record News*.)

It is thought by many that this is a picture of the first automobile in Wichita Falls, although the story cannot be verified. In any case, this is certainly an early vehicle. The year is 1907, and the driver is the owner, M. D. Walker. The car is a 1904 Orient Buckboard that Walker purchased for $450. (Courtesy of the Wichita Falls Museum of Art at Midwestern State University.)

Natural gas was piped from Clay County to Wichita Falls beginning in 1909. This crew, using both a Wichita truck and a horse-drawn wagon, are shown laying the gas line. Wichita Falls was the first city in the area to have access to natural gas. (Courtesy of the Wichita Falls *Times Record News*.)

William Jennings Bryan, one of the leaders of the Democratic Party, visited Wichita Falls in 1909 shortly after his defeat in the presidential election of 1908. Bryan is shown here sitting on the right in the backseat of the car. Driving is W. M. McGregor of the First National Bank. T. L. Tolen, principal of Wichita High School, is seated to the right of McGregor, and the Reverend W. F. Morrow, pastor of the First Methodist Church, is seated next to Bryan in the rear. (Courtesy of the Wichita Falls Museum of Art at Midwestern State University.)

The first streetcar went for a trial run on September 15, 1909. Frank Kell, who was instrumental in the development of the line, is shown standing near the front step of the car. Regular service began on September 16, 1909, and continued until July 4, 1934. (Courtesy of the Wichita Falls Museum of Art at Midwestern State University.)

The workers shown here are laying the track for the streetcar service that would begin in September 1909. (Courtesy of the Wichita Falls Museum of Art at Midwestern State University.)

Just after their Minstrel Parade on June 21, 1909, these Elks posed in front of the Wichita Opera House at 921 Indiana Avenue. J. N. Prothro stands third from the right in the back row. Others in the picture who can be identified are Butler Moore, Abe Marcus, Charlie Bean, J. W. Stone, Ed Gorsline, Walker Hendricks, and Mack Taylor. (Courtesy of the Wichita Falls *Times Record News*.)

Harvesting wheat could require a large crew of workmen, as shown in this harvest scene in 1910. (Courtesy of the Wichita Falls *Times Record News*.)

By 1912, harvesting had become mechanized, although in this picture the farmers are using both a steam-driven tractor and a horse-drawn wagon. (Courtesy of the Wichita Falls *Times Record News*.)

One of the first automobiles in Wichita Falls appeared in 1910. Seated in the vehicle next to the steam tractors are Joseph A. Kemp and Frank Kell. (Courtesy of the Wichita Falls *Times Record News*.)

The Wichita Falls Union Depot, built in 1910, was important to the city until passenger service was terminated in 1967. The following year, the depot was demolished. (Courtesy of the Wichita Falls *Times Record News*.)

By 1910, the population of Wichita Falls had reached nearly 8,000. Hence, the graduating class of 1911 was slightly larger than that of 1907. Note the beautiful gowns and hats these ladies are wearing. Their attire is an indication of prosperity. (Courtesy of the Wichita Falls *Times Record News*.)

The Wichita Motor Truck Company was organized in 1911 and operated until it was forced to shut down by the Great Depression. At the height of its operations, the company sold trucks all over the world. This picture shows one of the few Wichita trucks still in existence. Of course, it is not in very good shape. (Courtesy of the Wichita Falls *Times Record News*.)

J. J. Pontius, who called himself the "Flying Dutchman," came to town in 1911 to demonstrate his Curtiss biplane at the Lake Side Ballpark. The demonstration was a flop, for the aircraft never got off the ground. (Courtesy of the Wichita Falls Museum of Art at Midwestern State University.)

Here we see the Wichita Falls Police Department in 1912. Fred Smith sits proudly on their first motorcycle. The others are, from left to right, (seated) Chief R. V. Gwinn, Mayor Dr. J. M. Bell, and S. N. Jernigan, night chief; (standing) Andy Humphrey, Arthur Groves, Will Allen, Charlie Sommerville, unidentified, and J. P. Nail. (Courtesy of the Wichita Falls *Times Record News.*)

The village of Burkburnett, located about 14 miles north of Wichita Falls, was founded in 1907. The first bridge across the Red River into Oklahoma was this toll bridge located near Burkburnett. This photograph was taken in 1912. (Courtesy of the Wichita Falls *Times Record News.*)

The Noble-Frank Hardware Store was doing well in 1913. (Courtesy of the Wichita Falls *Times Record News*.)

This is the Wichita Falls High School graduating class of 1913. Regrettably their identities have been lost. Note that they are well dressed and some of them actually look happy. The gentleman at the left is superintendant McNew. (Courtesy of the Wichita Falls *Times Record News*.)

Some of the school buildings in Wichita Falls have been in service for nearly a century. In this photograph is Sam Houston Elementary School, located at 2500 Grant Street. It was built in 1913. (Courtesy of Annetta Reusch at Wichita Falls High School.)

In this Labor Day Parade in 1913, the horseshoers on the float shod seven horses between the time the event began and the time it ended. Anyone who knows anything about shoeing horses should be impressed. (Courtesy of the Wichita Falls *Times Record News*.)

This gas line crew is shown in action aboard their Wichita truck in 1915. (Courtesy of the Wichita Falls *Times Record News*.)

E. G. Hill, the undertaker, poses on the front steps of his establishment. The automobile at the right suggests that this photograph was taken in about 1915. Also note the gas meter at the left corner of the foundation. (Courtesy of the Wichita Falls *Times Record News*.)

This structure, located at the corner of Seventh and Scott Streets, was the home of Dr. S. H. Burnside. A graduate of the University of Pennsylvania, Burnside came to Wichita Falls in 1883. Among his early patients were Comanche Indians from the reservation near Fort Sill 50 miles to the north in Oklahoma Territory. Burnside also established the first hospital in Wichita Falls. In this picture, Mrs. Burnside is standing on the balcony, and the Burnsides' two daughters, Alice and Margaret, are seated on their ponies. Dr. Burnside stands between the girls, and Burnside's associate, Dr. Wade Walker, is on the right. The identity of the man on the bicycle is unknown. (Courtesy of the Wichita Falls Museum of Art at Midwestern State University.)

The Wichita Falls Sanitarium was the city's first hospital. Located at 716 Seventh Street, it was established by Dr. S. H. Burnside early in the 20th century and operated until 1915, when the Wichita Falls General Hospital was opened. Shown in this picture, taken in 1908, are, from left to right, Mrs. Burnside, Carvice Daugherty, Dr. Burnside, and Jim Walker with a dog. Nurse Lulu Daugherty stands on the upper porch. (Courtesy of the Wichita Falls *Times Record News*.)

Lake Wichita, created by Joseph A. Kemp's Lake Wichita Irrigation and Water Company by means of a dam on Holiday Creek, became a popular recreation site. The Lake Wichita Pavilion, pictured here, was built by Kemp and Frank Kell in 1909–1910. It featured a café and a skating rink on the first floor and a dance hall on the second floor. Eventually the recreation center included a hotel, summer cottages, a racetrack, a baseball park, and a penny arcade. Over the years, most of these structures were either dismantled or destroyed by fire. The last to go was the pavilion, which burned down in November 1955. (Courtesy of the Wichita Falls Museum of Art at Midwestern State University.)

The Circle Building at Lake Wichita was originally intended to be the site of the county fair but was used instead as a penny arcade. Nearby would be a merry-go-round and a Ferris wheel. (Courtesy of the Wichita Falls Museum of Art at Midwestern State University.)

This picture of Frank Kell (left) and Joseph A. Kemp was taken in their office in the Route Building, their headquarters, in 1915. By that time, they were at the height of their careers as businessmen and developers and were well-known throughout the Southwest. (Courtesy of the Wichita Falls *Times Record News*.)

Lake Wichita was a popular recreation site between 1902 and 1915. The Lake Wichita Trolley carried pleasure seekers from downtown to the lake, which was (and is) located on the far south side of town. (Courtesy of the Wichita Falls Museum of Art at Midwestern State University.)

Oilman Cy Bates (foreground) and a friend are seen here taking a keg of beer across Lake Wichita to their campsite on the south side of the lake. Bates is sitting on the keg. The year is 1915. (Courtesy of the Wichita Falls Museum of Art at Midwestern State University.)

Two

1915 THROUGH 1930

The occasional floods of the Wichita River, which flowed through the city, could be devastating. The flood of 1915 inundated most of the downtown area. Here some residents are seen boating on the 1100 block of Scott Street. (Courtesy of the Wichita Falls Museum of Art at Midwestern State University.)

In 1915, six Curtiss biplanes made the first cross-country flight by any military aircraft. They left Fort Sill and made their first stop in Wichita Falls on their way to San Antonio. They are seen here in a field near town. In the background can be seen a portion of the large crowd out to welcome them. (Courtesy of the Wichita Falls Museum of Art at Midwestern State University.)

Parmenter's Hardware Store was considered a state-of-the-art merchandizing center in 1917. Shown here standing under a bright light are, from left to right, Henry Parmenter, B. E. Parmenter, W. R. Little, Martin Standie, and Thomas E. Noble. (Courtesy of the Wichita Falls *Times Record News.*)

The oil well that started the Burkburnett boom was drilled on land owned by Shields Fowler in July 1918. Before it blew in, it was known as "Fowler's Folly" because most people predicted that it would be a dry hole. The drilling crew is seen here at the base of the well watching raw petroleum bubble out. (Courtesy of the Wichita Falls *Times Record News*.)

Another view shows workers at the base of "Fowler's Folly" in 1918. (Courtesy of the Wichita Falls Museum of Art at Midwestern State University.)

Oil field work was dirty, dangerous, and tiring. The men on this Wichita truck show their fatigue at the end of a day's work. (Courtesy of the Wichita Falls Museum of Art at Midwestern State University.)

This is Burkburnett at the height of the oil boom in 1919. There were no drilling regulations, so derricks could be seen everywhere, even in residential areas. (Courtesy of the Wichita Falls Museum of Art at Midwestern State University.)

By 1919, Burkburnett featured a forest of oil well derricks. The tanks in the foreground of this picture were used for the temporary storage of raw petroleum until it could be piped to the tank cars and transported to a refinery. (Courtesy of the Wichita Falls Museum of Art at Midwestern State University.)

Although there were no wells in the immediate vicinity of Wichita Falls, the city was nevertheless the center of the oil businesses. This view of Indiana Avenue in 1919 reflects the bustling prosperity of the time. (Courtesy of the Wichita Falls Museum of Art at Midwestern State University.)

During the oil boom and the business boom that followed, communications were important. Here is the Western Union office that was located in the Holt Hotel in the early 1920s. (Courtesy of the Wichita Falls *Times Record News*.)

While the oil business flourished, Wichita Falls featured five oil stock exchanges where large sums of money changed hands every day. This image is the Wichita Falls Central Stock Exchange on a typical day. The exact date is unknown but was probably sometime in 1919. (Courtesy of the Wichita Falls *Times Record News*.)

Oil fever brought so many people to Wichita Falls in search of wealth that housing was scarce. One solution was the creation of tent hotels like this one seen in 1919. (Courtesy of the Wichita Falls *Times Record News*.)

This was another tent hotel located at Ninth and Travis Streets. (Courtesy of the Wichita Falls *Times Record News*.)

As the search for oil expanded, several satellite towns sprang up near Burkburnett. All of them were very unpleasant places. In this photograph is the main street of New Town in October 1919. By that time, the village boasted a population of nearly 10,000 people, but like all the satellite towns, it declined rapidly with the end of the oil boom, and within a few years, it was gone. (Courtesy of the Wichita Falls Museum of Art at Midwestern State University.)

The discovery of oil brought the refinery business to Wichita Falls, and eventually there were 30 refineries in or near the city. Seen here is the Wichita Refinery, one of the smaller operations. (Courtesy of the Wichita Falls *Times Record News*.)

The Panhandle Refining Company was one of the first of its kind in Wichita Falls. It was founded by Roy B. Jones in 1918. The company's accounting department is seen here. (Courtesy of the Wichita Falls *Times Record News*.)

The Sunshine Refinery was another facility of this type in the Wichita Falls area. (Courtesy of the Wichita Falls Museum of Art at Midwestern State University.)

One of the more elaborate refinery plants was that of the American Refinery Company, shown here in the late 1920s. (Courtesy of the Wichita Falls Museum of Art at Midwestern State University.)

These gentlemen were part of the crew at the Wichita Valley Refinery in Iowa Park, a small town located about 15 miles west of Wichita Falls. (Courtesy of the Wichita Falls *Times Record News.*)

The truck seen here is being loaded with fuel oil for use in boilers in the oil field. Standing is Frank Daniel, and seated above is Bob Bradley. The year is 1917. There were already several wells in operation before the big boom of 1918. (Courtesy of the Wichita Falls *Times Record News*.)

Oil well fires were all too common in the oil patch. This photograph records efforts to put out such a fire in 1919. (Courtesy of the Wichita Falls Museum of Art at Midwestern State University.)

The Fort Worth and Denver City Railroad was busy during World War I and the oil boom. This photograph of the company's business office in Wichita Falls was made in 1918. (Courtesy of the Wichita Falls Museum of Art at Midwestern State University.)

The St. James Hotel was a favorite refuge of travelers in 1919. Here guests are seen relaxing in the lobby. Some were there so often that, according to local lore, the desk clerk knew them by name. (Courtesy of the Wichita Falls *Times Record News*.)

Although oil dominated the economy after the boom, agriculture was still important. The cotton bails seen here are waiting to be sold. The year is 1920. (Courtesy of the Wichita Falls Museum of Art at Midwestern State University.)

The wealth generated by the oil boom produced a building boom. This photograph from 1919 shows some of the major construction projects that were underway at that time. (Courtesy of the Wichita Falls Museum of Art at Midwestern State University.)

Another view of the building boom shows four buildings in the early stages of construction. From left to right, they are the Clint Wood Building, the National Bank of Commerce, a hotel, and the City National Bank and Oil Exchange. (Courtesy of the Wichita Falls *Times Record News*.)

Looking west on Eighth Street in 1919, one could see the early phases of construction. Eighth Street came to be known as "Skyscraper Row," although none of the buildings were true skyscrapers. (Courtesy of the Wichita Falls *Times Record News*.)

One of the more impressive structures that sprang up in the wake of the oil boom was the Clint Wood Office Building. Here it is seen nearing completion in November 1919. (Courtesy of the Wichita Falls *Times Record News*.)

The Palace Hotel, located at the corner of Eighth and Scott Streets, was demolished to make way for the Clint Wood building, which was completed in 1920. Wood sold the building to Bob Waggoner, who later sold it to the Wichita National Bank. This final photograph of the Palace Hotel was taken in February 1919. (Courtesy of the Wichita Falls *Times Record News*.)

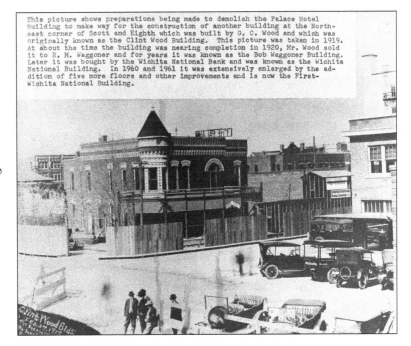

This picture shows preparations being made to demolish the Palace Hotel Building to make way for the construction of another building at the Northeast corner of Scott and Eighth which was built by G. C. Wood and which was originally known as the Clint Wood Building. This picture was taken in 1919. At about the time the building was nearing completion in 1920, Mr. Wood sold it to R. M. Waggoner and for years it was known as the Bob Waggoner Building. Later it was bought by the Wichita National Bank and was known as the Wichita National Building. In 1960 and 1961 it was extensively enlarged by the addition of five more floors and other improvements and is now the First-Wichita National Building.

This photograph, taken in the early 1920s, is a view of Eighth Street looking east toward the Union Depot. By that time, most of the major building projects in the downtown area were nearing completion. (Courtesy of the Wichita Falls Museum of Art at Midwestern State University.)

Call Field, a training center for combat pilots, operated in Wichita Falls from August 1917 to July 1919. Some of the Curtiss biplanes used for training flights are seen here lined up near the runway. (Courtesy of the Wichita Falls Museum of Art at Midwestern State University.)

Men on the ground watch intently as a pilot approaches for a landing at Call Field. Takeoffs and landings were extremely difficult because the planes were flimsy and had no instruments, and it was always windy. (Courtesy of the Wichita Falls Museum of Art at Midwestern State University.)

Crashes were common at Call Field. In fact, 34 cadets were killed in training. Fortunately, this pilot survived. (Courtesy of the Wichita Falls Museum of Art at Midwestern State University.)

This aerial picture of Wichita Falls was made by a Call Field pilot in 1918. The view is to the north. The downtown area is seen at the extreme right center of the picture, and the Kemp Mill and Elevator storage bins are at the lower right-hand corner. (Courtesy of the Wichita Falls *Times Record News.*)

Large crowds turned out to welcome the boys home at the end of World War I. This view faces east on Seventh Street toward the depot. (Courtesy of the Wichita Falls Museum of Art at Midwestern State University.)

This photograph of downtown Wichita Falls was taken in 1925 after most of the "skyscrapers" had been completed. Note that most of the automobiles parked along the street are Fords and most of them are black. The reason was that Ford's assembly line produced cars so fast that only black paint would dry quickly enough to keep up. It was not until 1926 that a new technology produced paint in various colors that featured a quick drying capacity. (Courtesy of the Wichita Falls Museum of Art at Midwestern State University.)

Wichita trucks were used for various purposes throughout the 1920s. This one was a bus. (Courtesy of the Wichita Falls *Times Record News*.)

The Union Depot, built in 1910, was busy for many years serving businessmen, travelers, ranchers, and farmers. Here are agricultural products ready for loading in the 1920s. (Courtesy of the Wichita Falls Museum of Art at Midwestern State University.)

Lake Kemp was built in 1922–1923 primarily for purposes of flood control. Interest in this project was triggered by the flood of 1915. Pictured here is the dam as it appeared in 1973. (Courtesy of the Wichita Falls *Times Record News.*)

Lake Diversion was built in the mid-1920s to add to the city's water supply. Seen here in 1961 is the dam on the Wichita River that creates the lake. (Courtesy of the Wichita Falls *Times Record News*.)

Madame Ernestine Schumann-Heink, the famous operatic contralto, visited Wichita Falls in 1920 and was treated to a rodeo. She is the lady in the center of the picture. Her reaction to the event is unknown, but clearly she is looking at the camera, not the horse. (Courtesy of the Wichita Falls Museum of Art at Midwestern State University.)

W. B. Hamilton was one of the city's most successful businessmen and developers. He built the impressive Hamilton Building in 1925, donated land for the Midwestern State University Campus, and was instrumental in the development of the Country Club section of the city. (Courtesy of the Wichita Falls Museum of Art at Midwestern State University.)

Mrs. W. B. Hamilton was one of the leading members of Wichita Falls society in the 1920s. (Courtesy of the Wichita Falls *Times Record News*.)

A popular attraction in the 1920s was auto racing. This photograph, taken in 1925, shows a racetrack at the site of Call Field. (Courtesy of the Wichita Falls Museum of Art at Midwestern State University.)

The Wichita Falls Spudders professional baseball team commenced play in the Texas League in 1920. The opening-day crowd filled the stands and then some. (Courtesy of the Wichita Falls Museum of Art at Midwestern State University.)

Although their numbers were dwindling, Confederate veterans continued to hold annual reunions. This one took place in Wichita Falls in 1920. The old gentlemen could still march. (Courtesy of the Wichita Falls *Times Record News*.)

The two Shriners in the front seat of this sleek roadster were enjoying carrying two ladies in the Wichita Falls Labor Day Parade of 1921. Unfortunately, the identities of all four riders have been lost. (Courtesy of the Wichita Falls *Times Record News*.)

Some of Wichita Falls' early settlers posed for this picture in the mid-1920s. Shown from left to right are (first row) N. H. Redding, Jimmy Batson, Mrs. J. A. Bradley, J. H. Barwise, Mrs. Ed Wilson, and R. E. Huff; (second row) W. J. Howard, Ed Wilson, W. T. Harris, J. A. Bradley, Mrs. A. H. Carrigan (daughter of J. H. Barwise), J. C. Ward, and T. G. Stevens; (third row) Henderson Bates, John Taylor, Eddie Williams, Ed Suddeth, and Ben Williams. (Courtesy of the Wichita Falls *Times Record News*.)

This handsome Victorian building served as the Wichita Falls High School from 1890 to 1922. It was demolished in 1928. (Courtesy of the Wichita Falls Museum of Art at Midwestern State University.)

Memorial Auditorium, located on Seventh Street just west of the downtown district, was built in 1927 in hopes of attracting conventions and major entertainers. This photograph was taken in 1930. Wichita Falls did not become a major convention center. (Courtesy of the Wichita Falls Museum of Art at Midwestern State University.)

On December 12, 1929, the Antlers Hotel burned down. Three people, including two firemen, Smiley Turner and G. L. Anderson, were killed. (Courtesy of the Wichita Falls Museum of Art at Midwestern State University.)

The Weeks Mansion was built in 1924–1925 by lawyer William Fred Weeks, who arrived in Wichita Falls in 1910 fresh out of Yale Law School. Weeks prospered and became active in civic affairs. He donated land that became a park in the center of the city and supported the Spudders baseball team. He suffered financial difficulties during the Great Depression, and in 1932, he moved to Tyler, Texas, where he began anew and prospered once again. For many years after Weeks' departure, the house sat vacant or was used as a restaurant, a private club, or home to the city's little theater. Recently, it was purchased by a local family and is once again a private residence. (Photograph by the author.)

In this photograph of downtown Wichita Falls taken in 1932, the new post office is under construction. On the far left is the First Methodist Church, and in the center background is the Hamilton Building. (Courtesy of the Wichita Falls Museum of Art at Midwestern State University.)

For many years, the Wichita Club, formed by local oil men, was located on the 11th floor of the Hamilton Building. Pictured here is a banquet that took place in the late 1920s or early 1930s. Note that most of the ladies are wearing hats, which was customary at the time. (Courtesy of the Wichita Falls *Times Record News*.)

Frank Kell established the Wichita Mill and Elevator Company shortly after his arrival in 1897. It soon became the largest business of its kind in the Southwest. His Wichita Falls facility is shown here as it appeared in the 1930s. Kell had sold the business to General Mills in 1928. (Courtesy of the Wichita Falls *Times Record News*.)

On June 14, 1929, this Ford tri-motor inaugurated the Safeway Airlines service at Wichita Falls. Prior to that, the Wichita Falls Air Transport Company had made occasional flights to Dallas and Fort Worth. Braniff Airlines also had extended service to Wichita Falls in February 1929. (Courtesy of the Wichita Falls Museum of Art at Midwestern State University.)

The Western Air Express began service to Wichita Falls in April 1930 with this Fokker 12-passenger tri-motor. The city's airport at the time was known as Kell Field. (Courtesy of the Wichita Falls Museum of Art at Midwestern State University.)

Hoping to find oil at deeper levels, a group of Wichita Falls businessmen formed the Deep Oil Development Company. Their first well blew in at the Chalk Hill field on March 23, 1931. Eventually 40 wells were developed in the Chalk Hill area. The Deep Oil Development Company leaders were Jack Kadane, Fred Kadane, Preston Wood, J. M. Hagger, Charles Kadane, L. W. Mangold, Edward Kadane, L. C. Griffith, G. Dillard Anderson, and George Kadane. (Courtesy of the Wichita Falls Museum of Art at Midwestern State University.)

The Great Depression did not prevent Wichitans from celebrating their Golden Jubilee in 1932. Pictured here are Lester Jones (left), chairman of the jubilee's historical committee, and Walter Cline, chairman of the entire celebration. Cline was one of the partners in the Fowler well project. (Courtesy of the Wichita Falls Museum of Art at Midwestern State University.)

Three

1930 TO THE PRESENT

This image shows John G. and Mary Hardin as they appeared in the 1930s. At that time, the Hardins were donating large sums to educational institutions, including Midwestern State University. Another of their beneficiaries was Hardin-Simmons University in Abilene. (Courtesy of the Wichita Falls *Times Record News*.)

The Women's Forum was organized in 1924. Its headquarters building, shown here, was built in 1930. The forum was and is dedicated to literary attainment, social enjoyment, and "the betterment of the physical, intellectual and moral conditions of both the individual and the community." (Courtesy of the Wichita Falls *Times Record News*.)

Many celebrities visited Wichita Falls during the 1930s. Pictured here are Gordon W. "Pawnee Bill" Lillie and his wife, May Manning Lillie, posing with Mayor John T. Young (center) in 1932. Pawnee Bill was the owner of a popular Wild West Show. (Courtesy of the Wichita Falls Museum of Art at Midwestern State University.)

Jess Willard (center), a famous prizefighter, is shown here with Lester Jones (left) and an unidentified man. Willard visited Wichita Falls in 1934. (Courtesy of the Wichita Falls Museum of Art at Midwestern State University.)

These people were the ground-breaking ceremony committee for the new Post Office Building in April 1931. Standing just to the left of center is Ed Howard, publisher of the city's two newspapers. (Courtesy of the Wichita Falls Museum of Art at Midwestern State University.)

James V. Allred served as district attorney of Wichita County from 1923 to 1928. He was attorney general of Texas from 1933 to 1934 and governor from 1936 to 1939. He was a Democrat and an avid supporter of President Roosevelt's New Deal programs. (Courtesy of the Wichita Falls *Times Record News*.)

The last service at the First Methodist Church at Tenth and Lamar Streets took place in 1931. The building was demolished to make way for the new Post Office Building. (Courtesy of the Wichita Falls Museum of Art at Midwestern State University.)

Wichita Falls' business district still appeared to be prosperous in 1931. Although the impact of the Great Depression hit Texas a little later than other areas, it would eventually take its toll in terms of business bankruptcies, unemployment, and other features of hard times. (Courtesy of the Wichita Falls Museum of Art at Midwestern State University.)

These gentlemen were members of the Exhibit Committee in the Golden Jubilee of 1932. Standing at the far right is Lester Jones, the chairman of the committee. (Courtesy of the Wichita Falls *Times Record News*.)

The last streetcar ride in Wichita Falls took place on July 4, 1933. Many local celebrities participated, although no individuals among the passengers posing for this picture can be identified. (Courtesy of the Wichita Falls Museum of Art at Midwestern State University.)

Although streetcar service ended in 1933, the demolition of the tracks did not begin until 1935 and the task was never completed. Some tracks are still visible today. (Courtesy of the Wichita Falls Museum of Art at Midwestern State University.)

During the drought of the 1930s, dust storms were common. This one struck the area in 1936. Such storms were dangerous. Not only did they destroy farmland, they could also be very unhealthy. (Courtesy of the Wichita Falls *Times Record News*.)

John Hirschi began farming in Wichita County in 1888. He later went into the real estate, investment, and oil business, where he prospered. During the Great Depression, he held 400 mortgages and refused to foreclose on any of them. Instead, he cut interest rates, reduced principles, and extended amortization periods. (Courtesy of the Wichita Falls *Times Record News*.)

This portrait of Hirschi was made near the end of his life. He died on January 29, 1950, at the age of 93. A real estate firm bearing his name still exists in Wichita Falls. (Courtesy of the Wichita Falls *Times Record News*.)

Mrs. Joseph A. Kemp, widow of one of the city's most prominent developers, posed for this portrait in 1956. (Courtesy of the Wichita Falls *Times Record News.*)

Joseph A. Kemp's home was located at Tenth and Grant Streets. In this image, it appears as it did just before it was demolished in 1960. (Courtesy of the Wichita Falls *Times Record News.*)

Mrs. W. B. Hamilton continued to be active in local affairs for many years after her husband died in 1962. (Courtesy of the Wichita Falls *Times Record News*.)

Mrs. Hamilton occasionally served as the engineer of a miniature train located at Funland, a small amusement park located on Southwest Parkway. Funland was demolished in 1999. (Courtesy of the Wichita Falls *Times Record News*.)

The home of W. B. Hamilton, successful oil man and former mayor of Wichita Falls, stands at 1100 Brook Street. It was built in 1918 and purchased by Hamilton in 1932. Today the house is home to law and business offices. It was placed on the National Register of Historic Places in 1983. (Courtesy of the Wichita Falls *Times Record News*.)

With the Route Building in the center and the Holt Hotel in the background, this image reflects the trash that remained after the destruction of the Union Depot Building in 1968. (Courtesy of

the Wichita Falls *Times Record News*.)

The People's Ice Company began business in 1912 and continued to operate until 1969. In this image, at about that time, owner Al Cobb stands with some of his machinery and several hundred pounds of ice. (Courtesy of the Wichita Falls *Times Record News*.)

Lake Arrowhead, built in 1968, is today the main source of water in Wichita Falls. Located about 10 miles south of the city, it is also an important recreational site, as seen here. (Courtesy of the Wichita Falls *Times Record News*.)

The tornado of April 2, 1958, struck a residential area of the city and did substantial damage. In this image, the funnel is about to touch down. (Courtesy of the Wichita Falls *Times Record News*.)

This photograph reflects some of the damage wrought by the tornado of April 2, 1958. This storm killed two people and injured many more. (Courtesy of the Wichita Falls *Times Record News*.)

The tornado of 1964 struck the north side of the city and did substantial damage to Sheppard Air Force Base and the nearby residential area. (Courtesy of the Wichita Falls *Times Record News*.)

In addition to major property damage, the tornado of 1964 killed seven people. (Courtesy of the Wichita Falls *Times Record News*.)

The tornado of 1979 was the worst storm to ever strike the city. It developed around 6:00 p.m. on April 10 and traveled across the city, destroying many homes and businesses, killing 42 people, and injuring hundreds. It was one mile wide. (Courtesy of the Wichita Falls *Times Record News*.)

People stand in awe and shock as they observe some of the damage caused by the tornado of April 10, 1979. This photograph was taken on April 11, 1979. (Courtesy of the Wichita Falls *Times Record News*.)

Midwestern State University moved its campus to its present location on Taft Boulevard in 1936. This image reflects its appearance in 1947. Several of the buildings on the perimeter of the campus are old barracks moved from Sheppard Air Force Base. (Courtesy of the Wichita Falls Museum of Art at Midwestern State University.)

Hardin Hall is the main building on the Midwestern State University Campus. In it are the administrative offices and some classrooms. Hardin Hall is named for John G. Hardin, who contributed large sums of money to the support of education. Built in 1936, it was the first structure on the new MSU campus. Pictured here is the main entrance of the building. (Courtesy of Midwestern State University.)

This image captures the beauty of the main quadrangle at the west side of Hardin Hall at Midwestern State University. (Courtesy of Midwestern State University.)

The president's home on the campus of Midwestern State University was built by Louis Sykes, a local oil man, in 1940. It was turned over to the state in 1974. Although it is not an exact copy, its style is based on Mount Vernon, the home of George Washington. (Photograph by the author.)

Midwestern State University provides superior housing for its students. Here a group of them relaxes on the porch of an apartment in Sunwatcher Village. (Courtesy of Midwestern State University.)

The Dillard College of Business Administration is a major feature of the Midwestern State University campus. (Photograph by the author.)

Kay Yeager, a major player in the city's business community for many years, has served as mayor of the city and on the board of regents of MSU. Her hard work resulted in the Multipurpose Event Center, which includes an exhibit hall, an agriculture center, and a coliseum. The coliseum features numerous entertainment events and is the home of the Wildcats, Wichita Falls' hockey team. The coliseum is named in honor of Yeager. (Photograph by the author.)

This home at the corner of Buchanan and E Streets is an example of the houses built by oil men immediately after World War I. This one was built was in 1920 by Jasper Ferguson, who hoped to replicate a French chateau. The portion of the house at the left is an addition built in 1963. The house is located in the Floral Heights District, the first area of the city chosen by the oil men as the site for their homes. (Photograph by the author.)

This was the home of Roy B. Jones, who came from Oklahoma to Wichita Falls to establish one of the early refineries. Built in 1927, the house is located in the Morningside District, the second area of the city chosen by the oilmen to establish their homes. (Photograph by the author.)

This handsome structure, built in the 1920s, was once the home of oilman Walter Cline. Although not an exact replica, it is patterned after the White House, home of the president of the United States in Washington, D.C. (Photograph by the author.)

In the 1970s, the Wichita Falls Bureau of Commerce and Industry aggressively recruited businesses to locate in Wichita Falls. One of the results was the arrival of Washex, a manufacturer of commercial washing machines. (Photograph by the author.)

Pittsburg Plate Glass is another of the major industries brought to Wichita Falls by the efforts of the Bureau of Commerce and Industry. At the time of its construction, this was the world's largest and most modern float glass plant. It is capable of producing one million feet of glass a day, most of which is sold to window manufacturers. About 25 percent of the production is sold to automobile and other commercial manufacturers when times are good. (Photograph by the author.)

The Kemp Library was built by Joseph A. Kemp and donated to the city in 1918. Today it is the home of the Wichita Falls Center for the Arts. (Photograph by the author.)

The queen of all the office buildings in downtown Wichita Falls is the Hamilton Building, erected by W. B. Hamilton in 1925. It is located at the corner of Eighth and Lamar Streets. (Photograph by the author.)

A reminder of one of Frank Kell's successful businesses, this grain storage facility is still in use even though the business office building at the right has been allowed to deteriorate. (Photograph by the author.)

Wichita Falls High School, known to most residents as "Old High," was built in 1923. The early classes of Wichita Falls Junior College, eventually to become Midwestern State University, were held here. Today Old High is one of three public high schools in the city. (Photograph by the author.)

The Wichita Falls Post Office Building, built in 1932 during the Great Depression, is still in use today. In addition to the post office, it houses several federal offices. (Photograph by the author.)

Where once the streets of Wichita Falls were very unattractive, today they feature numerous ornamental structures, such as this one at the corner of Midwestern Parkway and Hamilton Boulevard. (Photograph by the author.)

This street ornament at the corner of Kemp Boulevard and Scott Street commemorates the tower on the Union Depot, which was demolished in 1968. (Photograph by the author.)

Until recently, Wichita Falls had few attractive parks. Today it features Lucy Park, a popular site for picnics, exercise, and relaxation. (Photograph by the author.)

This sculpture by the great artist Jack Stevens commemorates the Native Americans who roamed North Texas before the coming of the white settlers. It is located on the bank of the Wichita River on the east side of the city. (Photograph by the author.)

The "Littlest Skyscraper" was built during the oil boom. It was financed by investors who believed they were supporting the construction of a full-sized building. They were swindled. Today it is a landmark and a monument to the city's past. (Photograph by the author.)

The Route Building was built in 1909 by Frank Kell and Joseph Kemp. It was the site of their business office for many years. In 1992, it was purchased by the Wichita County Heritage Society, and more recently, in 2007, it was sold to an insurance company. (Photograph by the author.)

The cornerstone of the Route Building commemorates the many contributions of Frank Kell and Joseph Kemp to the economic and social development of Wichita Falls. (Photograph by the author.)

Recently, the Museum of North Texas History acquired a flyable Curtiss "Jenny" of the type used to train pilots at Call Field during World War I. This building is the home of the Jenny, which is taken out for a brief flight once each month. (Photograph by the author.)

This monument was originally located at the site of Call Field. Today it stands at the doorway of the hanger that houses the city's Curtiss "Jenny." (Photograph by the author.)

The Wichita River never had a true waterfall, although there were rapids that were destroyed in 1886 when a dam built by waterpower enthusiasts washed out. A century later, the city built an artificial waterfall, which was first turned on in 1987. The opening ceremony gained national attention. The mayor of Niagara Falls, New York, sent a commemorative rock, and the dedication was featured by NBC's *Today* program with weatherman Willard Scott officiating. The bridge seen here at the base of the falls spans the Wichita River and is part of a popular hiking and biking trail. (Photograph by the author.)

The Wichita Falls, unlike most natural waterfalls, can be turned off and on. Here are the falls in the off position. (Photograph by the author.)

This is the public entrance to Sheppard Air Force Base as it appears in 2009. Sheppard was first opened in 1941, closed temporarily at the end of World War II, and reopened in 1951. It is a major contributor to the economic and social structure of Wichita Falls. (Photograph by the author.)

Sheppard Air Force Base has always welcomed visitors from the community. This image captures an open house in 1960. The people in line at the center of the picture are waiting to tour the interior of a B-52. (Courtesy of the Wichita Falls *Times Record News*.)

During the cold war, Sheppard Air Force Base was home to B-52 bombers of the Strategic Air Command. They were capable of flying over the North Pole, attacking a potential enemy on the other side of the world, and returning to their base. (Courtesy of the Wichita Falls *Times Record News*.)

Sheppard Air Force Base in Wichita Falls was one of several sites housing Titan Intercontinental ballistic missiles during the cold war. They first arrived in 1960 and were removed in 1992. Fortunately, it was never necessary to launch them. (Courtesy of the Wichita Falls *Times Record News*.)

Visit us at
arcadiapublishing.com

Printed in the USA
CPSIA information can be obtained
at www.ICGtesting.com
LVHW070148221123
764347LV00058B/1030